Most gratefully dedicated to my family.

"Like a Mustang,

*Imagination is wild and free.*"

©Heather McGowan 2015

# Contents

Introduction - Publishing my first poetry collection

## My Story
### The Original Collection

## A Mother's Day
### Collection

## Inspiring
### Nature & People

~~~

# Introduction

For so many years I have written poems to share with my closest family members and people in my life. In more recent years I have used my blogsite to share my work temporarily in my "Poem of the Month" section and occasionally posting via social media to gain instant feedback. Due to my keen interest in music and song writing from my schooldays, many of my poems have become songs which I play alone at home or in trustworthy company. The first time I shared a song (Little Bird Song) to a large audience was at my wedding, where it was used as a soundtrack for the video I dedicated to my husband as a quirky means of sharing vows. From this experience I received so much positive feedback from friends and family, whom many of which were shocked to discover that I could sing.

Publishing my poems has been suggested to me and a dream I've held onto for over 12 years, when I first began collecting my poetry. To actually be writing this section of a book seems so surreal to me, even though I've always been a writer. I also feel that at this point in my life, as I carry our first child, publishing my poems is certainly a milestone of success to mark the end of the first chapter of my life as I enter the exciting, unknown wonderful world of parenthood. The name of the first and main section of this book *"My Story – The Original Collection"* is named accordingly to reflect the story of my first "life chapter" and I suppose it only felt right to publish this collection when I knew the first chapter was over- until now, it was not clear to me what that was.

My poetry is primarily inspired by nature. Most of my poems are either about nature or use metaphorical messages of the natural world to create a piece of writing that more readers can relate to as they are invited to interpret my work through their own perspective. I also feel that descriptions of the natural world make words so much more visual and beautiful to read; as I feel so connected to nature, I believe that by writing about the earth's natural habits, I can clearly communicate my inner world onto paper as the most accurate expression of my thoughts and theories.

The first and main section of this book has already been explained briefly- I just wanted to complete this introduction by explaining my reasons for the structure of my collection. *"The Original Collection"* is in chronological order from my first poem I saved in 2006 to my latest work in 2018 where I experience an introduction of the very intense mothering instincts during pregnancy. Although specific people were in mind at the times these poems were written, I can still relate the words to my current, loving and secure relationships I have today.

*"The Mother's Day Collection"* is a collection of poems I have written on various Mother's Days over the years. Quite often my own mother would not wish me to buy her a gift, but would look forward to something I have written for her to express my gratitude of her being there. I have also, in the main collection, a poem I have written for my father on Father's Day as well as a tribute to both my parents. I feel that having a mother's collection is important to me as I, myself will become a mother and having that reminder of all the inspiration, in the form of my poems which I wrote for my own mother, will help me out during those challenging times ahead.

Finally, the miscellaneous section. *"Inspired by Nature & People"* is a small collection of poems I was inspired to write randomly by certain people or experiences and realisations about nature. This section is not in chronological order yet specifically ending with *A Natural Story*- an early poem I wrote outlining the positives and negatives of each season but how each trait has its own beauty. I felt this would be a perfect note in which to end my first collection and leave the reader feeling closer to having a respectful view of our natural world and perhaps closer to understanding me as a writer.

I write for myself and the way in which I write comes entirely from within and with some methods, I simply can't explain how I came up with the words but I can explain why they are there. I wanted this initial collection to be completely authentic and original therefore all my poems are written the way in which they were at the time of creation. Any changes of wording or additional alternatives given at a later date were done so by myself only to accommodate song lyrics or a new rhythm. The images for my poetry were also designed by myself. Many of the poems in this collection are written for certain people in my life and I would like to thank those individuals for standing out to me and having multiple inspirational aspects to inspire me for different poems. You know who you are and if it wasn't for you, then I would not have the unique collection of poems I have published in this book today.

Thank you for purchasing a copy of this book- your support really means a lot to me at this stage. I invite you, as the reader, to interpret the words of my poems as personally as you wish. I hope you find my poetry enjoyable and inspirational so please take from it what you will.

"I do not run alone,
They're all here beside me...

They want
what I want...

And they're all deep
within me..."

©Heather McGowan 2015

*Heart of a Mustang, page 12*

## The Last Ride

My heart was always warm,
When you were there to greet me,
I would see you standing tall,
Gentle shadow watching over me.

With eyes so kind, you looked to me,
A look of hope, returned, you'd see,
Dreaming of times where we would ride,
And never have to say goodbye.

As I would brush away your dust,
Inside, I'd always feel your trust,
You'd always stand so calm and still,
Yet when we're free, you gave me thrill.

I look to you, so tall, so proud,
Magnificent, you steal the crowd,
As I mount, on this dull day,
I fear the fate,
Which caused these skies to grey...

As we walk the dusty land,
Forgetting everything,
Time comes to a stand...

Here, behind your flowing mane,
I urge you on, I whisper your name,
As steady you turn,
Steady, you flow,
Steady, you fly,
Steady, you ride...

I feel your flow,
Right through my bones,
I hear your breath,
As you carry me home,
And the drumming below,
Goes on... and on...
Like the beats, of my heart...

As time goes on, we have to part,
I wish we could go back to the start,
Time goes too fast, it hurts my throat,
My tears are lost in your glossy coat.

I dream that you would carry me,
So far away, so fast, so free,
The drumming in my heart goes on,
Just wishing you were never gone,

...Because in my dreams, you're always there,
A gentle friend here for my care,
In my dreams, you're never gone,
We're forever riding, on and on...

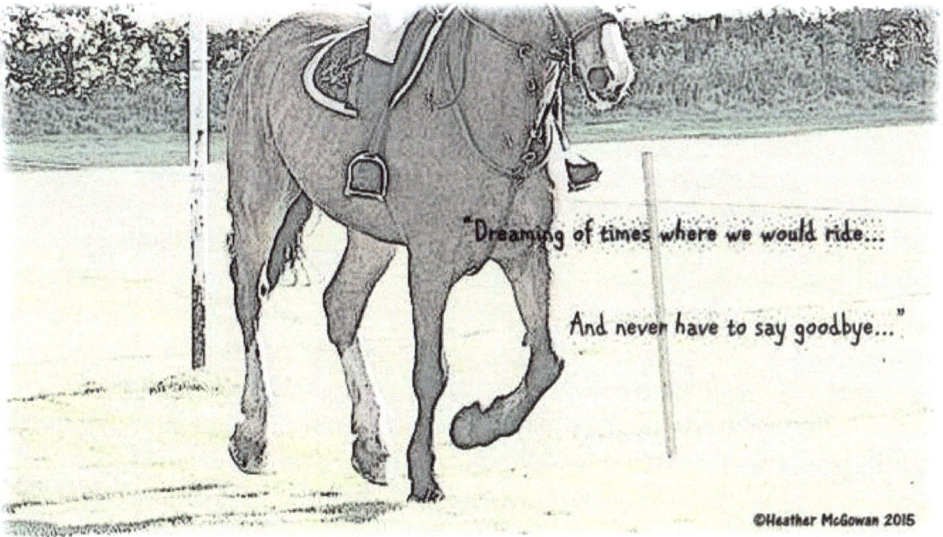

"Dreaming of times where we would ride....

And never have to say goodbye..."

©Heather McGowan 2015

**The Shadow Men**

Good night me love, they allus' say
Sleep tight n' keep those bed bugs away

Time to shut thi eyes and dream
An' hope this night don't end wi' a scream

Now we're off on the Midnight Express
Destination, Panic Station n' runnin' on stress

We can't hold back, no time to delay
Now the Shadow Men's on their way...

They'll feed on fear, turn you to stone
They make it clear, you're on your own,
Whispers threatening in your ear
Shadows gettin' near and near
Now they'll eat your ripened fear.

What's that you say, it's just a dream?
Well me dear, that it may seem...
But why is it, I don't hear you scream....

Good night me love, sleep tight in bed,
Watch the Shadow Men, within thy head...

GOOD NIGHT ME LOVE,
SLEEP TIGHT IN BED,

AND WATCH THE SHADOW MEN
WITHIN THY HEAD...

## Motivation

"Back with vengeance!"
My Sensei told me.
And he would not be wrong...

I was only a germinating seed back then,
Only just planted,
I did not seem to break off the path,
Just focused on one straight line.

I got a flying start, my keen mind kept me running,
But my roots had not sunk deep enough,
I then slowed to a stand-still...

I had not the strong branches which now surround me,
They grow out and keep me standing.

From the little shrub I once was,
We are now a steady tree,
We sink deep in the toughened turf, impossible to up-root,
We blossom when times are good,
We shed leaves when they're bad,
We are forever growing,
Our water in an everlasting supply,
Forever welcoming new trees to the forest.

"Back with vengeance!" my Sensei told me.
And that I'll always be.

## Magnetic North

Left with my heart all black and blue,
Thought I'd never love again, until I met you,
Moulting indoors, light vanished from my eyes,
He drifted from me, unaware of my cries.

I'd struggle for height in the wide open sky,
At least with your smile, I was able to fly,
You lit up my eyes when you could not see,
Then I saw how much you cared for me.

Moving on through clouds, a little lost swallow,
But something within told me what to follow,
They always wonder, but fail to say,
How a migrating swallow can find their way.

Sometimes small feelings would hold me back,
But so I could reach you, I'd fight through the flack,
Nothing is stronger than natural forces,
They're bound tight together, like a herd of wild horses.

This one thing within me, pushed me to go forth,
This compass directing me magnetic north,
Through all of those feelings, when I could see clear,
To be with you is natural, we've nothing to fear.

## Tomorrow

In your eyes there's a man,
Who does what he can
To make it through those times that are rough.

In your eyes there's a past,
But you won't let is last
Cos' you know to put it all behind.

In your eyes there's a girl,
Walking by your side
And she's here, listening to you...

In your eyes there's a key,
To a house by the trees
Where young birds, learn to spread their wings.

I know that one day,
When the sun shines her way,
Through the clouds and the mists that divide,
I know that one day,
The sun will shine her way,
Over fresh green meadows,
And more...

In your eyes there's a girl,
Waiting for the time,
When she never has to say goodbye...
But she knows, until this day,
We must keep fighting on
Never, never looking back...

**You Were There**


As I fought through my last days of high school,
Battling with both time and stress,
When this feisty young falcon within me,
Frustratingly screamed to escape the nest in which she was imprisoned,
School gates like bars of a cage, watching the free world around her,
Her wings are mature, but the flight she seeks is forbidden.
As she longed for the day when horizons afar seem so much nearer,
You were there.

When I studied miles from home,
Returning to my home town in darkness,
So many tasks, so little time,
As this fledgling climbs higher up the face of the cliff,
Still sheltered by a crevice, which keeps out the storms of the outside world.
As she fought the mighty sea gales, trying to tear her wing,
You were there.

As I reached times of decision,
Does she fly? Does she hide?
To take flight and patrol the blue skies is her dream,
Her strong, swift mate by her side,
But so many forces try to push her back to the nest,
She just follows her will, no looking back.
As she parts from others and takes flight,
You were there.

Now, I am astray in the big wide world,
As this young falcon ascends into blue skies,
Soaring higher each and every day,
Alone?
She is timid and adventurous, but never alone.
As she ventures into the tough world around her,
You were there.

Moving on, forever wandering, forever traveling,
Other fledglings remain protected,
So much routine, so many expectations...
When my fledgling is shot down, she is damaged,
But she knows she will be stronger next time,
She knows because you were there...

And she knows she will patrol her skies proudly, someday,
And as others look up to her,
She knows she will never be alone,
She knows because, you will be there.

**Little Blue**

In this little blue stone,
Through your blue eyes,
I see tomorrow,
With no goodbyes.

With this little blue stone,
Glistening clear,
Dreams of tomorrow,
Seem so much nearer.

Blue is the sky,
On a crystal clear day.
Blue is the ocean,
Calmly seeping into the bay.

Blue is content,
Blue are your eyes,
Blue lights the way,
To clear blue skies.

**Innocent Mind**

It started with a fight.
Once a perfect picture, reflected in the lake,
Nestled in a calm and content valley,
A clear, precious crystal they promised to cherish,
Forever...
But what was this promise, to an innocent mind?

And when the crystal shatters,
The glass cuts deep, through fair, fresh skin.
Bleeding goes on for days and nights, and years...
Dark, red stains seep through satin,
The stains remain forever.
"If only they had stayed together"
An innocent mind prays.

A falling tear, screams in the night,
The wild cats hiss and screech downstairs,
Tearing each other to shreds...
They fight in a cold, midnight dessert,
Leaving that lush, perfect world behind them,
Following the dusty path.
Haunted by the distance and misunderstanding,
Leaving crystal, shattered, in their wake...

It ended with a fight...

## Heart of a Mustang

The wind in my long, entangled mane,
The fear of isolation in my deep, dark eyes,
How when I am alone, I just go insane,
As the wild mare within, I obey her cries.

At dawn or dusk, I stray up the hillside,
Windswept, I watch over what is before me,
As I start to run, from the world I now hide,
Through the woodland and meadows, at last I am free.

I push and I push 'til my vision is hazy,
No one is there and nobody knows,
I don't even care, if I'm totally crazy,
This is just what I do, through the highs and the lows.

I do not run alone, they're all here beside me,
They want what I want,
And they're all deep within me...

If ever they see, if somehow they know,
How I get my thrills for what I am grieving,
Maybe someday, I will move on and grow,
Unless this heart of a Mustang just keeps me believing...

*"Like a Mustang, imagination is wild and free"* – H.Judd

## Angel

Falling for a heart,
Beyond my powers to heal,
Misreading my path,
Ignorant, to what is real.

Trapped, with my heart,
Longing to be free,
Lost in a trance, blinded,
From what others could see.

Tied, a drift, under a spell,
A voice deep within cries,
It cries all night long,
Why do you listen to these lies?

I will not be broken,
I live to be free,
I've heard the voice of an Angel,
I know who I want to be...

I race for my future,
My past lays in the dirt,
I listen to my Angel.
Knowing I won't be hurt.

## Sixth Sense

Hearing you cry in the dead of the night,
Seeing through your eyes when there is no light,
Feeling your touch as you ease the pain,
I still taste your lips, when you are far away,
Your scent surrounds me from day to day...

Like the trees need the Fall to shed their leaves,
How the spider has enough silk as she weaves,
Like clean, pure water from bubbling springs,
How little birds know when to spread their wings...

...And know just where they need to be,
How they work together like you, with me,
Strongly connected, like the root to the tree...

Like the flow of pure water, so fast and intense,
Like your mind, within mine,
Like you are my sixth sense.

**Butterflies**

Symmetrical, colourful are our butterflies,
Forever bright and playful, as time passes by,
On silken wings, they dance with ease,
And flutter in the Summer breeze,
Waltzing to a distant twitter, of birds within the trees.

A delicate wing, so soft and petite,
Satin armour, solid against the winds they meet,
Strong and courageous are our butterflies.

Nervous, quivering, alert of all around,
Twitching at a shadow, or subtle, distant sound,
Cautious, intelligent, innocent are our butterflies...

They dance in the sun as their wings a-glisten,
The beats drumming faster as we listen,
To our bright, symmetrical and beautiful butterflies.

**Beautiful**

Through the darkness of the trees... there is light,
The rushing stream can shimmer... with a sun beam,
Once a forest of hidden nightmares,
Threatening eyes lurking behind branches,
Upon me, a timid little thing


Hiding behind my heart,
Blind to the mysterious beauty out there,
Too stubborn and innocent to let go and explore


I'd lost my passion,
I'd lost myself.
And then, suddenly,
I was alone.


My world, once a shimmering crystal,
Now a shattered mass in the dark
Forced to let go,
Yet still, I stood proud.


I took a step towards the forest,
As I heard a wild mare cry,
I heard the sounds of a whisper,
I felt it was worth a try...


My crawl swiftly accelerated, I began to run,
As I saw the glimpse of her red coat glisten,
A wicker through the leaves,
As she turns her head to listen...


I called to her to mend my heart,
She led me through the trees,
I followed, trusting every step,
Leaves surround me in the breeze.

Deeper and deeper into this woodland,
For so long, forbidden to me,
Through their beautiful kind eyes,
At last, I could finally see...


Through the darkness of the trees, here is my light,
A hidden beauty, revealed, and I am not afraid,


As I stand within the core,
With this beautiful mare,
On this beautiful, lush grass,
Beneath these beautiful trees,
On this beautiful day,
Looking into your beautiful, kind, blue eyes.

## Little White Rose

My Brothers, you have always watched over me.
Maybe I have not always appreciated your magnificence,
As you stand there, looming across the rigid landscape,
Blocking out the sunlight.


It is only when I stand upon your shoulders,
I feel the freedom you share with us,
No matter how impossible it may seem,
It is always worth the struggle to join you.


My Brothers, why is it you are still there?
When I want to see beyond your great mass?
Why must I climb every time, I wish to feel like a free bird?
When I am caged, not nestled, under your immense shadows.


I have a call within me, Brothers,
A distant cry for lands where I can see for miles,
Where I can feel as free as wild Mustang on the Great Plains,
A land which gives me the urge to run with the wind...
Brothers, I have found this land:
The roads are open, and so are my eyes,
The rivers are calm, as are my nerves,
The fields spread for miles, as does my mind...


For in this place, I can think, feel and run,
The air fills my lungs with inspiration,
I spread my arms and at last I have won,
Nature has found me a new creation,


No mountains to hold me,
Just the wind blows,
I lay among willows,
For my Little White Rose.


*For my parents, who gave me the White Rose.*

## Little Bird Song

I found a little bird
Singing sweetly from the ground,
Such a soft little bird
I held in my hand.


This innocent little bird
He followed me home,
Such a tired little bird
But what a beauty you are.


I cleansed the little bird
So much dust on his wing,
Learn to fly little bird
Because, how sweetly you sing.


Take flight little bird,
From the treetops you sing,
You were my little bird,
Such a brave little thing.


I held the little bird
So much trust he had in me,
Aim high little bird,
Fly high and be free...


*For my inspirational husband, Dean- The little bird who found his own wings.*

## Dear Cherry Blossom

Dear Cherry Blossom,
As I open my eyes, in this season of joy,

Ready for the beginnings,
As are your pretty pink buds,
I know I am blessed this and every springtime,
When your subtle and still nature accompanies my smile...


Hearing your whispers in the wind gives me warmth,
I feel secure in your branches,
I am thankful for each and every one of your vines,
For they are all precious and there for support,
Without them I know I surely would fall,
I have climbed so high to this day...


I remember the times I would stay on the ground,
Dancing among your sweet petals,
As they flit and flutter around me
They fill me with such melodic gratitude...

Now are the days where I climb to my nest,
High up, in the safety of your canopy,
I am grateful for your kind power to hold me,
Yet trust that I will not fall...

For you are the reason on this earth,
For my healthy heart,
Mind, Body and Spirit,
You have blessed each part of me.

Tree of power, inspiration and life-giving spirit,
You allow me the best in this world,
For my happiness is yours.

Thank you, Cherry Blossom,
Your most grateful & blessed hatchling.


*A letter of appreciation and gratitude to my family, for their continuous support,
throughout the life changing experiences that come with moving away from home.*

## Child of Nature

I needed no game boy,
I played out alone,
I needed no electronic cyber pet toy.

Let me run wild,
Escape to the trees,
Knee deep in rivers, a true nature child.

My playlist is bird song,
I have no ipod,
For nature is music and I dance along.

The wind in the trees,
The coo of a dove,
A twitter of finches, the humming of bees.

For this is my life song,
My true company,
I don't feel alive in the city too long.

Police sirens squeal,
Drunk youths bawl,
I flinched every time, like there was some big deal...
Did not like the way I was beginning to feel...

Now I have found my inner peace,
I have escaped once more,
I followed the pathway to my release.

Feeling familiar natural air,
Grass beneath my feet,
Wind entangling my wild, curly hair.

This was all worth fighting for,
For me to be with myself,
Where I can run so freely, be a child of nature once more...

## Mountains Divide Us

I knew from the start,
Since we live apart,
That mountains will divide us.

We need to be strong,
Believe it won't be too long,
Until they no longer divide us.

Click-eh-dee clack,
Through the Peeks and back,
Huge boulders that divide us.

From East to West,
Longing for a nest,
With no mountains to divide us.

From the big city lights,
To magnificent sights,
Over mountains that divide us.

Before we did leave,
Since we met one late eve,
We had mountains to surround us.

We now stand alone,
Each to our own,
It's only mountains that divide us.

## All I Need

All I need is the sunrise,
At the start of the day,
And the warm colours in my heart,
To wake me up, where I lay.

All I need is the meadow,
Fresh grass beneath my own feet,
With all the space I need to run,
Like the stallion, I greet.

All I need is the rainbow,
At the end of the storm,
To flow with the colorus within my heart,
And to keep dry, and warm.

All I need is the forest,
A whispering breeze in the air,
And all the tall trees to shelter me,
To hold me, keep me aware.

All I need is the moonlight,
That pearly light in the sky,
Shining upon the right paths for me,
And guiding me, from up high.

All I need are the flowers,
The bird song within the trees...

And all I need is the wind to blow,
For the energy,
To flow...

Then I will see, the true me,
As the birds, trees and wild flowers do,
With all the energy from this earth,
Unconditionally, so do you.

... And now all I need is a way to show,
That I see the true you, too.

*A Father's Day poem- for a Dad who showed me the true beauty of nature.*

Blue is content
Blue are your eyes

Blue lights the way
To clear blue skies

I held the little bird,
So much trust he had in me...

Aim high, little bird,
Fly high and be free...

© Heather McGowan 2013

**Unbroken**

Easy, easy don't shake your wild mane
For I heard your cry in the dark
Steady, steady let's not play the game
I hear, yes! It's no walk in the park.


Hush now, hush for you have my ear
I see the look in your eyes
You light the fire to hide your fear
And take on this feral disguise.


Pawing the ground, tossing your head
And now they are under attack,
You won't stop 'til contentment is fed,
You struck when they turned their back.


You searched for a forgiving spirit
That lifeline who would never give in
For they can see what's behind it
They want nothing but for you to win.


The forgiving compliments the fighter.
Water puts out the fire.
The darkness turns much lighter.
And everyone meets their desire.

**In Waves**

What is to be said for us now, dear friend...

Since we shared that tight, bonding, quick-release knot?

Our voices aloud are a no man's land,
However, is it the norm when I hear that calling,
Staring out at sea, watching the deep, dark waves...

As I walk along the sand in the cloudy, moonlit beach,
I hear it in the waves, as they rapidly lap up the pebbles,
The mist distorts my vision, as I can't quite make out,
If it's you I can hear, or just my inner challenge...

Whatever I feel,
Whatever I hear,
I know it comes in waves,
Whenever I see,
Whenever I call out,
I know I'm drowning in waves.

For as long as I'm aware,
I can find my fins and share,
For I know it only comes in waves...

**Some Day**

You were born in my heart.
Your most graceful gaits accompanied each gait of my life,
Our paces harmonize in perfect symphony.

You gave my excitement.
As a child, I was born under you,
I found my dreams within you,
Embracing your peaceful aura, I fell in love.

You gave me sanctuary.
When storms pushed me beyond my path,
I found myself within you,
Under your eyes of empathic kindness, I healed.

You gave me hope.
In this challenging mission of life,
I found my power because of you,
For your eternal presence, I am driven.

All my life,
I dream of our hearts merging,
To form a raging river,
And as one, we will ride.

We will ride together,
Breathe together,
And hold each other,
Someday...

## Our Christmas Eve Song

Silent night,
Christmas Eve night,
The sea was calm,
The town, all bright,
Round the harbour, swans bathed in moonlight,
Streets so empty, no soul within sight,
As we walked by the shore,
Knowing our era was born...

Christmas Eve night,
Beginning is nigh,
One more hour,
In your sight,
Not meant to stay out beyond midnight,
Yet, in that moment, fate told me I'm right,
To stay in your arms all the way,
Til' morning on Christmas Day.

Silent night,
Christmas Eve night,
Four years passed,
All, still bright,
Radiant beams fall upon our lives,
Binding together, our family unite,
For Christmas evening is here,
That most wonderful time of the year...

*For Dean on our four year anniversary of being together.*
*24/12/16*

## Write From The Heart

For so many years I've wondered,
What it is I am to do,
So many years spent wasted?
And productive years are few?

How am I to get ahead now,
And use what I have inside,
Put these words of thought onto paper,
From the voices in my head...

As I try to piece together,
What it is they have to say,
Am I going round in circles,
Or is this the only way.

Sometimes what it is,
You need to make your way,
To do a bit of something,
You know is going to stay.

For me, this isn't my passion,
Not even something new,
It's just a little skill I know,
Just something I can do.

So many people turn their passion,
Into ways to earn their pay,
But for me it ain't that easy,
Work is just another day.

Putting my heart and soul into someone else,
Just to be buried in the past,
That is not the way I roll,
Now I won't let this last.

As I try to piece together,
What is it I am about,
Is this just another phase,
Or have I found my own way out?!

Write from the heart,
It's what I learned to do,
Right from the start,
It's always what has seen me through.

## Be Feral

When you hear a strange sound in the midst of night,
When your gut says there's something behind you,
Although, when you look there is nothing in sight,
Then you know you got to be feral.

When your heart skips a beat in that moment,
When you know that somethings not right,
All of your senses seek that movement,
From you to the one that is feral.

When a stranger gives you a suspicious look,
In their eye you detect signs of madness,
To retreat from being trapped by a crook,
You know it's time to be feral.

For to be feral is to be conscious.
To be feral is under-rated.
To be feral is to have your instinct.
To be feral is to protect.

Be feral to fight,
To stay, hide,
To take flight.
Be feral for you are alive!

Do you hear, that sound in the night?
Do you listen to your third eye?
Do you ever trust a stranger?

Or are you afraid to be feral?

## Ghost

I see, within my own eyes, your ghost
Haunting my reflection...
In my dreams, your ghostly whispers,
Fill my head with distant promises...

I just keep striding on as you follow,
Hand-in-hand with my spirit...
Fearing your presence,
I am slave to our immortal connection.

In the warmth of the Sun, I can dance all day,
Yet, when the Moon is risen,
Her cold light glistens in your deep, blue eyes...
Feeding my repressed, undead suffering.

Once my Angel, showing me light,
Now you haunt me night by night,
What is this unfinished business?

I know, to you, a debt is owed,
For only then, I can let you go,
Rest in peace, I've heard your cries,

Now it's time to close those faithful, kind, deep, blue eyes...

For this Ghost is always in this tense,
Triggered, like a long lost, sixth sense...

## Is That Really Tea?

I remember, like it was yesterday, not 6 years ago today,
It was just another night on the town with friends and my lad,
Time to "let our hair down" for the weekend "get the drinks in",
Everyone's youthful obsession...

I remember, like it was yesterday, not 6 years ago today,
While we were all drowning in spirits, while the room was buzzing,
There you were across the table,
Fingerless gloves gripped around a mug of tea...

I remember, like it was yesterday, not 6 years ago today,
My first words to you, after you caught my eye:

"Is that really tea?"

The shock in my voice, not shocked that it was actually tea,
But shock to my soul to see a guy so free,
And so content to just be...

I remember, like it was yesterday, not 6 years ago today,
Your heavy, dark hair over your crystal blue eyes,
Your quirky piercings in your lips and nose,
Head to foot in black with an arm of colourful tattoos,
You were an inspiration to me from this moment...

I remember, like it was yesterday, not 6 years ago today,
The way you hunched, timidly on your seat, almost in fetal position,
Ironic, for the beam of confidence and positivity,
You projected onto me that night,
From this moment I was subconsciously hooked, drawn to you...

I remember, like it was yesterday, not 6 years ago today,
That on that night, after those brief words,
I'd carried on my normal, insecure life- a prisoner to love,
And slave to my stubborn, loyal heart,
With no idea that I had just visited my future.
A glimpse into the light,
Before following my path into the shadowy forest for another night...

I remember, like it was yesterday, not 6 years ago today,
That when I looked into those hidden blue eyes,
There was something about you,
Something about your crazy hair,
Your cool, grungy clothes and pierced lip,
Your colourful mass of tattoos and little tea-clutching hands...

Something inside me knew,
There was more to this timid, petite guy,
Sitting in the pub across the table that night.
Something that, although the room was full of people,
Laughing, drinking and my friends catching-up,
For that brief moment, you had every little ounce of my attention...

I remember, like it was yesterday.
I could not be more grateful for that moment, on that night,
6 years ago today,

For not only do I have that memory,
I have your wedding ring,
Your name,
And your child,
And that amazing thing about you, in my life forever.

And I could not be happier, that I asked you:
"Is that really tea?"

*An ode to the unforgettable night I met the "Tattooedteabag".*

**Little Conker**

Dear little conker,
Inside your silken shell,
A ripening little beauty,
An incredible story to tell.

Precious little conker,
Within your satin skin,
Your heart and soul of solid oak,
Nestled in a thorny layer, you spin.

Fierce little conker,
Your fiery will to grow,
Let's the whole world know you're here,
Nothing will stop your flow.

Forgive me, little conker,
For wishing time away,
I just can't wait to meet you,
And nestle you myself, one day.

Inspiring little conker,
For beneath your silken skin,
You hold the power to change our world,
For our exciting new chapter, is about to begin...

Round the harbour
Swans bathed
in moon light

Streets so empty,
Not a soul within sight

As we walked by
the shore,
Knowing
our era was born...

Forgive me little conker
For wishing time away
I just can't wait to meet you
And nestle you myself
One day

## A Prayer For Spring

So brave, you face him, strong,
Blinded by his power,
To never surrender,
The stone cold pure heart, of Winter.

Even when his days are numbered,
He has the upper hand, and ways,
To send in his Snowflake Soldiers,
Each so soft, such beauty they behold...

Yet once they're armed and ready,
And turn from few to many,
Covering ground from far and wide,
From beneath that frosty exterior, you hide...

Your beautiful pastel Tulips shiver,
Sunny Daffodils, they quiver,
While Crocus and Snowdrop, they stand tall,
Peaked above this great snowfall.

You will not allow this beast,
To manipulate his Winter feast,
For he just points that icy finger,
A challenge, to prolong his days and linger...

But you have youth upon your side,
Possess your own beauty and pride,
Send in the fury of your fleet,
Until this meltdown is complete!

Oh, Summer Sun, beyond the skies,
As she nears the Earth, she hears your cries,
Casting Sun Beamers upon the land,
It's time to make your Springtime stand!

Once pure white, now faded grey,
Now the Beamers have their way...
His icicles will shed their tears,
For the only thing that Winter fears...

Her early rises, her radiant light,
Her late departure into the night,
Her perfect storms, her April shower,
From Summer Sun, you will seize her power,

For once his icy grip is thawed,
He no longer holds his frosted sword,
He bows his head and waters run free,
Stubborn, holding on, though he's down on bended-knee...

Young, green buds burst their way,
Into arms of Sun Beamers, to dance and play,
The Blackbird carves his nest of art,
Awaiting new life and Springtime to start.

Surrender now, Winter, you desperate fool!
Begone with your blizzard cloak, your eyes deep and cruel,
For your days are now over,
Retreat, to your dark, cold cavern...
Await Autumn's calling,
For now, we're through, young Spring's day is dawning.

Now Summer Sun has taught her lesson,
As a mother's daughter accepts her blessing,
At last, painting your canvas in peace,
A long, warm breath of colour, you release.

Giving life to every tree,
To birds and flowers, for the little honey bee,
Giving light to extend the day,
And warm up the Earth, for offspring to play.

Spring bares laughter, Spring bares hope,
Spring eases our stain and struggles to cope,
In her colour and beauty, we share her fun,
Right from Spring Day til' she becomes our Summer Sun.

## Little One

Dear Little One,
Hear me as I hold you close,
Closer than I ever will again.

Talk to me, Little One,
As I feel your heartbeat,
Louder than I ever could before.

Move for me, Little One,
Tell me in your own way,
Let me know that you are well once more.

Just keep kicking, Little One,
You can never hurt me,
Be strong, be curious, be here.

I long to meet you, Little One,
And look into your eyes,
Until that day, I swear to you,
I'll just keep holding you closer...

## The Blackbird Song

Morning star of the dawn chorus,
He stands beaming from the tree top,
Welcoming the colourful day before us,
With his ebony feathers and delightful hop.

Hear that cheerful distinct melody,
As the Sun ascends Eastern skies,
Delivering his musical remedy,
That warning chatter as he flies.

Content, submerged in his glorious sound,
In his waves I am carried along,
Welcoming you to this earthy ground,
To the beautiful Blackbird song.

# ~ The Mother's Day ~
## Collection

"As I graze alone in the fell top mist,
Being looked upon by a ram...

I learn what she learned,
I know for myself,

That she was once, a Little Lamb..."

©Heather McGowan 2015

*Little Lamb, page 44*

## Mother Nurture

A whole childhood, nestled, in the whisper of the wind,
A gentle breeze,
Floating through innocent leaves.
The leaves you held,
So comforting in your robust arms,
Knowing not what you did,
Yet so sure, following your heart...

Such a huge heart,
Beating within the wings of shy hummingbird,
So fragile, so small,
Yet her joy, glowing for miles all around her,
Love sharing, in her sweet nectar...

Nectar so pure, so rich, saved for her crystal,
Her little seedling, buried deep underground,
A mighty acorn, bursting with spirit,
Fed only through the minerals of Mother Oak's deep root...

A root so strong, so tough,
No storm nor machine could ever unearth,
For the will of Mother Nurture has more power, more intent,
Than anything man's most naive mind could invent.

Her will to survive,
To deliver,
To grow,
Devoted to her seedling, so fiercely bound...

A seedling so tiny,
Filled with instinct and potential,
Strives to receive,
To follow,
To grow...
To grow with the wind,
Through the leaves,
And up the root,
From that deep, rich underground cavern,
To break through her shell,
To show her strength, as she now stands in clear view,
Striving with Mother Nurture,
To be a Mother like you.

For my own inspirational Mother on the first Mother's Day I had the earliest experience of motherhood itself as I grow my own little seedling, 2018.

**Spring is Just Around the Corner**

It's seven AM,
The sun has risen,
We'll soon escape this Winter prison,
Soon the trees will grow their leaves,
And swallows will drift in the mild breeze.

The first young lambs huddle in plastic jackets,
They bleat and crinkle like potato chip packets,
The winds still howl and rain still pours,
As yet the Summer sun still snores.

We walk through fields, ankle deep in slush,
How mild Winter rain kept grass green and lush,
The big brothers of hills admire the land,
As nimble old ramblers, struggle to stand.

Soon the clouds will part away,
And bitter cold winds will be astray.
It's seven PM
And not yet dark,
There's action on at Derwent Park.

*Mother's Day 2008*

**Little Lamb**

I opened my eyes as I began to shiver,
Clambering up on my wobbly pins,
A cold force pushed me, all a-quiver,
I hear the cries of my bleating twins.

I look up, and there is mother,
I shelter in her cozy wool,
Without her here, I would suffer,
For she'll get me through this Winter lull.

As she feeds me, it tastes nice!
It warms me up inside my tummy,
Until I forget about the snow and ice,
All I think about is mummy.

As days go by, as I play and hide,
With my friends I am free all day,
But I'll always end up by Mother's side,
And always listen to what she will say.

On the move again, on the mountain side,
And I stray from Mother again,
I keep my distance from walkers, as they stride,
To battle up the ledge in the rain.

Mother has taught me who to trust,
I know soon, I will wander alone,
And feeding myself is a must,
But I know Mother will never be gone.

Now I graze alone in the fell top mist,
Being looked upon by a Ram,
I learn what she learned, I know for myself,
She was also once a Little Lamb.

*Mother's Day 2010*

## Hummingbird

From whom does Hummingbird secure her joy?
Who put the colours in her wing?
Where did she learn to feed on sweet nectar?
Gaining the best from everything?


As she flits from petal to petal,
Beating with joyous energy,
How did she learn to share her love?
Sweet as sweet, pure honey?


And as she sings her morning chorus,
Little birds hear her song,
For she knows how to open her heart,
For others to sing along...


Such a big heart a little bird,
But from where did she receive?
From whose nest of feathers did she raise?
And learn how to believe?


Hummingbird is joyful,
Hummingbird can fly,
Hummingbird is thankful,
For the brightness in her eye.


*Mother's Day 2015*

# ~ Inspiring ~
## Nature & People

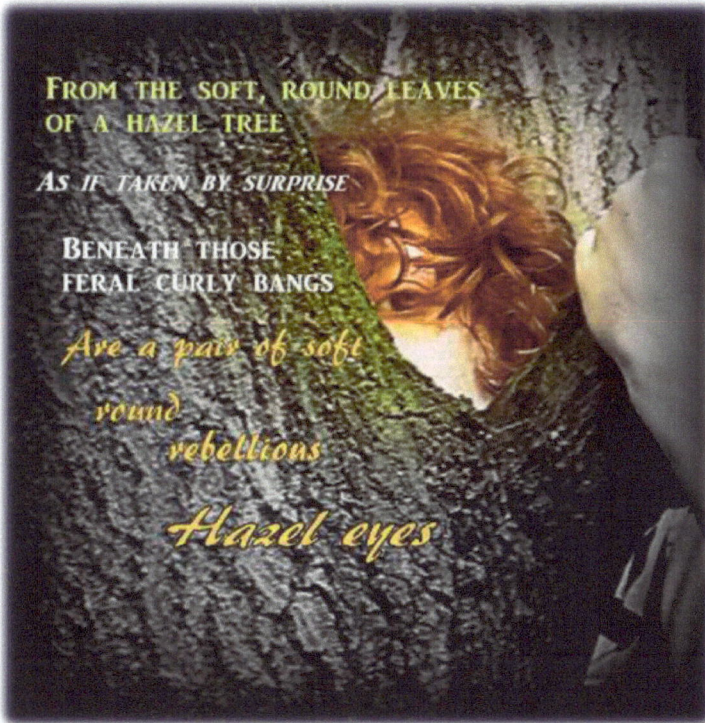

FROM THE SOFT, ROUND LEAVES
OF A HAZEL TREE

AS IF TAKEN BY SURPRISE

BENEATH THOSE
FERAL CURLY BANGS

*Are a pair of soft*

*round*

*rebellious*

*Hazel eyes*

*My Hazel, Page 50*

### Beautiful Babe

Opening your eyes to a glistening new world,
Surrounded by sunshine and love,
As colourful birds take flight from canopies,
You see them soar freely, above.
Welcome home, beautiful babe.

You hear waves striking the shore with power,
Then inhaling the rich golden sand,
Music all around you, from day to day,
Mum n' Dad sing along, hand in hand.
Come listen, beautiful babe.

Such a robust little soul, you have,
One day, with the strength of a brumby, you'll run,
To take on the ocean, to climb the trees,
Joining motley birds in their chatter and fun.
Live long, beautiful babe.

How radiant your days will be, little one,
A most tropical world around you,
So many worlds lay beneath your shell,
An incredible story within you.
Follow your spirit, beautiful babe...

*For an inspirational couple, Cristiana & Jay- written for their little Eddie, born 2016.*

## Peaceful Mind

There is a place where a stream trickles gently through sheltered woodland,
Flowing over pebbles creating soft, tiny bubbles,

There is a place where birds sing in perfect harmony,
Where a Tree Creeper leads her mate, as they dance around branches.

There is a place where sounds of the outside world can only be heard at the pitch
of a whisper...

And in this place hangs a tree swing,
Hanging by a knotted, faded white rope,
Ends cut off, all tatty...
Hanging with the memories of past times it has fulfilled,
They seem like only yesterday.

The trees around me stand tall and strong,
Forever our childhood faithful playmates,
In this place they keep me safe...

This is my place, but is open to you,
There are just the trees, the birds and me,
And all those pleasant memories...

## We Play by Moonlight

As we play by moonlight,
Other children sleep tight,
They have played in the sunlight,
They're back indoors at night.

We dance under stars on frosty grass,
We don't have no school or class,
Our colours are blue, silver and white,
As we play by the cold moonlight.

We are ghosts as we scream and shiver,
We are carried along by our icy river,
Always taken in before the rising sun,
Before the flames take over and end our fun.

Winter, our friend, he holds no threat,
When we open our eyes, the sun is set,
As Summer dominates our outdoor life,
The pain, if we'd step out, cuts like a knife.

We hide indoors as we hear them play,
Longing to join them 'til the end of the day,
But the Summer sun threatens to take our site,
If we don't stay inside and play by moonlight.

**My Hazel**

In the depths of the forest, calm and still,
Not a glimpse of a critter in sight,
The twitter of songbirds, chiff and chaff,
From the realms of the dim woodland light.

From the rush of the river, a trickling stream,
To the rustle of the wind through the leaves,
Was that, but a creek, of an old elm branch,
Or distant croak from a raven's throat, as it deceives.

In the depths of the valley, of the nature's child,
A wildflower grows within the trees,
A sweet heart of nectar she sings, like the birds,
In an onyx shell she whistles along with the breeze.

She runs with the heard, observing like a hawk,
Taking flight, they will carry her home,
Her will to run, her will to heal,
Their empathy forbids her, from ever being alone.

In the depths of the forest, calm and still,
Beyond the distant humming wings of flies,
From the soft, round leaves of a hazel tree,
As if taken by surprise,
Beneath those feral curly bangs,
Are a pair of soft, round, rebellious hazel eyes.

## October Moon

On a cool, clear night,
Watching over me,
Is a beautiful, shining, pearly light.

With a gusty, Autumn breeze,
Glowing so strong,
You really are "a ghostly galleon, tossed on cloudy seas".

Breathless, I look up to you,
Phantom of the skies,
A powerful silver aura, almighty, you shine through.

Following me, wherever I go,
Angel in the darkness,
Watching you in early fall, as night by night you grow.

With deep regret, I'll turn in soon,
Yet, at least I'll know, As from tonight,
I will sleep tight, under a beautiful, bright October Moon.

## A Natural Story

As the icy wind slaps you in the face, leaving it feel tight and tingly,
As the little Robin huddles away under the garage roof, safe from the blizzard outside.
When the swallows no longer sweep through the air,
Air so dry no bee or blue bottle would ever survive...

As darkness falls when lights are out, a beautiful silence harmonises through the night,
The pure white land presents pictures of shimmering waves, creating natural light,
Dancing flakes sprinkle from the moonlit sky, a most magical scene,
The sharp cold air steels your breath... if it is still there...

As pure white snow turns to ugly grey slush, making your socks all soggy and wet,
When April showers fall, and early lambs are drenched like drowned rats.
Miserable grey skies haunt the landscape, threatening to empty with hail,
Too cold to go out, too bored to stay in, the sea is as angry as you are...

Yet as the weeks move on, when the sun breaks through the clouds,
Her golden rays gently lighten the nights, and open up bright merry daffodils,
Mild clean air welcomes swallows and swifts, as they roost by the fire-lit sky,
Colourful dragonflies greet the first lilies, bobbing on sparkling waters.

As the sticky heat is upon us, drying sweat leaves a nauseating stench,
Sweltering with no clouds, no shade from the increasing blaze of the sun,
The torch in the sky creates idleness, everything is an effort,
Slugs and snails shrivel up and sizzle on the big, hot, dry griddle...

But gentle trickling streams cool your feet, happy ducks swim alongside you,
Lush green grass in the shade of the trees, with a songbird's melody around you,
A tired old mare lies quietly, swishing her mane and tail in a continuous rhythm,
The sun sits peacefully on the horizon, sinking softly in the warm, orange glow.

As the summer sun packs up her light and warmth, moving on her way,
Leaving you with darkening nights, October mist and a chilly breeze,
The swallows have now long gone, they've escaped the driving rain,
  Hibernating hedgehogs are tucked up in their burrows, now the cold is on his way...

But the pretty autumn colours collect at the foot of trees, shiny coats of horse chestnuts peep,
And as the leaves are falling, a most divine confetti display appears,
Clear, November night skies twinkle with far away stars,
An owl shrieks in an old oak tree, her silken feathers glimmering in the moonlight...
Just as beautiful as nature can be...

# Special Thanks

I would like to firstly thank my amazing family, who have been there to read and listen to all my poetry I've gathered throughout the years- I value your feedback more than anything and if you hadn't been there to support me, I doubt I would have even considered publishing. Thank you to my parents Richard & Annis, my Grandparents Shirley, Eric & Maureen and of course my inspirational husband, Dean. You have all given me so many reasons to write over the years.

I would also like to thank my close friends who have given their personal feedback and for being so supportive. I would particularly like to thank my friend, Laurel, who suggested to me the title of this collection and since then I couldn't think of anything better!

I would also like to thank my English teacher from school, Mrs. French. We lost touch years ago but if it wasn't for your guidance during the GCSE English Literature years, I wouldn't have developed my passion for poetry and creative writing which has stayed with me for many years, even if it was just in the background for most of the time.

I would like to thank my Dad once again and my friend, Stacey of Pixie's Photography for providing several of the image I have used to edit for this book.

Finally, I would like to take this opportunity to express my gratitude for the natural world we live in and how Mother Nature, herself, is enough to inspire a whole poetry collection from my own imagination. I believe respecting nature and the universe means kind things happen to us in return when the time is right. I am certain that my inspiration from nature is limitless and our natural world will continue to assist my creativity for many more years to come.

# About the Author

Heather Judd (previously known as Heather McGowan) was born in a small coastal town called Whitehaven on the edge of the Lake District in Cumbria, North West England, UK. Heather grew up here as an only child and was very close to her family, establishing close relationships with her parents and grandparents, who all lived locally and were hugely supportive of her writing since she was at school.

Heather has always been inspired by nature and a keen writer, writing only in her free time and only sharing her work with close friends and family for many years. It was only when she left her home county in 2014, that she decided to branch out with her writing and experiment with other styles other than poetry and creative writing, starting a blog in January 2016 while she was still at university, living in Manchester.

Heather met her husband, Dean, back home in 2012 who became a huge inspiration for Heather's poetry; they are now happily married, living together in North East Derbyshire in a small village just outside the city of Sheffield where Dean had studied Creative Arts Practice at university. Heather and Dean both left Cumbria to study in 2014 at separate universities. In April 2016 Heather moved to Sheffield to live with Dean in their first apartment. Heather left her counselling studies the following October and found work in Sheffield while she contemplated what to do with her career.

The whole time Heather was at university and after moving to Sheffield, she was gradually rediscovering her childhood passion for writing and life events continued to inspire her growing poetry collection as well as her lifestyle blog. Heather always knew she wanted to work for herself and even during her university studies, she discovered life coaching and began studying an adult learning program to learn coaching skills, which helped her personally and professionally.

In late 2017, Heather and Dean discovered they were expecting their first child and, when she was well into her pregnancy, Heather had decided that motherhood was her new motive to finally do something she enjoyed while being a new mother. Heather aspires to combine her passion for writing with her newly found love for coaching to one day earn a professional income for her new family, working from home. This was the point in which Heather decided to publish this first poetry collection, which had been hidden for over 12 years, before her life changed forever as this positively overwhelming new chapter begins.

Content submurged in his glorious sound
In waves I am carried along
Welcoming you to this earthy ground
To the beautiful Blackbird song